How to BAG A BUNNY

A DATING GUIDE FOR MEN

KARI NAUTIQUE

Columbus, Ohio

How to Bag a Bunny: A Dating Guide for Men

Published by Gatekeeper Press
2167 Stringtown Rd, Suite 109
Columbus, OH 43123-2989
www.GatekeeperPress.com

Photographer: LM Photo, Luis Munoz

Notice of Non-Affiliation and Disclaimer

ISBN (paperback): 9781662903083
eISBN: 9781662903090

CONTENTS

Prologue   What is a Bunny?............................ 7

Chapter 1   Healing Your Traumas................. 15

Chapter 2   Establishing Friendship 31

Chapter 3   Be Your Best Self........................... 41

Chapter 4   How Fast is Too Fast?................... 49

Chapter 5   Love Language and
             Body Language............................. 59

Chapter 6   Don't Be An Asshole..................... 77

Chapter 7   Perfection is Subjective................ 99

Chapter 8   Understanding the
             "Creep" Factor 109

Chapter 9   Building a Strong
             Relationship and Keeping It!......... 119

Chapter 10   Accepting Your Bunny 137

Chapter 11   Digital Dating............................... 145

Chapter 12   Compatibility and

               gulp "Zodiacs" 153

Chapter 13   Taking Constructive

               Criticism 159

Chapter 14   Hop To It! 167

Chapter 15   Direct from the Bunnies 175

PROLOGUE

What is a Bunny?

Who am I to give you advice on love?

I am someone who has been through a lot of shit. I am also someone who will be able to give you enough insight to keep you from going down some of the paths of failure that myself and others have gone through.

Although my views on love and dating have evolved,

the definition of a "Bunny" has stayed the same for me throughout the years. When the idea for this book originally came to me, I was working closely with Playboy Enterprises in Los Angeles and spending my weekends at Hugh Hefner's home. I became friends with the many women who earned the title of becoming a Bunny. Consequently, a lot of my friends back home asked me to introduce them to all my new friends. I knew right away that these women were out of their league, but not on a physical level.

Of my friends who were asking, none of them were emotionally mature enough to "Bag a

Bunny." The women I met were a different breed. I am still in awe of them, not because of their external beauty, but because of their personalities. They were some of the kindest, most inspirational, motivating women I had ever met. A Bunny, to me, is a smart woman with her head on her shoulders, a sense of class, and a heart of gold. If you are lucky, she'll come with a dark sense of humor, too.

So when I say, "How to Bag A Bunny," I'm not promoting a book on how to pick up women. Please notice how there's no "n" in the word "Bag." This isn't a hook up book or how to pretend to be someone you're not to impress a bunch of models.

This book isn't meant to be picked up, read in one sitting, and never touched again. My hope is that this advice will help your love life grow, and you will learn something new every time you come back to it. It is about being confident in yourself and your abilities. It is about developing a deep and meaningful relationship with the Bunny in your life; the person who makes your heart skip a beat and inspires you to be the best version of yourself.

Originally, when I came up with the idea for this book, I had no idea what I was talking about. Reading through my old manuscript and research from 2012-2015 was like a giant slap in the face. It was shallow, accusatory, and narcissistic; however, at the time, so was my relationship. What I thought was real love was actually an abusive and damaging relationship in the long run. It led to my own depression, alcoholism, anxiety, low self-esteem, and unsuccessful overcompensation.

Thankfully, after years of doing it the wrong way, I was able to escape that façade and focus on some much needed healing and growth. After discovering what doesn't work, I then sought therapy, read countless dating books and blogs, and interviewed successful couples. I feel like I am now finally able to construct a book to help others have the successful and healthy relationship of their dreams.

I wish I could go back in time to that unloved version of myself and show her how damaging and narcissistic that form of "love" was to her. I wish I could show the old me what real love should feel like and how to achieve it. I can't help my past self, but I can help the future relationships I have. I can also help you develop yours as well. Lastly, this book was written to help us achieve a long-lasting relationship. It will also teach us how to overcome our past insecurities, in order to gain the confidence to move towards healthier relationships.

Hop to it!
Xoxo,
Kari Nautique

CHAPTER 1

Healing Your Traumas

I used to live in this really small apartment in New Jersey. I loved everything about it, except it had a wobbly dishwasher. You see, the appliances were new, but the dishwasher wasn't installed properly and was entirely unbalanced.

If I pulled the bottom rack out all the way, it would tip forward and the door would bang on the floor... this happened every time I would load it or unload it. All of the dishes would roll forward slightly and the silverware would clang against each other. It was the most loud and annoying sound, and it startled me every time it happened.

I called a maintenance worker to come and check it out, and after an insane bill and nothing fixed, I was told to be careful when I rolled out the bottom rack. For the entire year I had lived there, I was afraid of the dishwasher rocking forward. No matter how gentle I was, the damn thing would still slam forward unexpectedly and uncontrollably.

Thankfully, the very next place I moved into didn't have that problem. In fact, I've never lived anywhere since that had an off-balance-dishwasher problem like the one I had in that apartment. At first, it was just a habit to be gentle when I would load or unload the dishes, like walking on eggshells. If I accidentally pulled it too far forward, I would become startled out of the sheer expectation of the loud clanging of dishes and silverware when the door hit the ground… except, it didn't happen. I had a perfectly safe and reliable machine, capable of quietly and effectively doing its job.

Over the next year or two of living in that new place, I

gradually became comfortable. I stopped thinking about the dishwasher at my old place, and eventually forgot about it entirely.

I lived my life. I washed my dishes, and nothing bad ever happened in dishwasher-land.

However, that doesn't mean that I still didn't occasionally *think* about it happening again. I still had residual anxiety that one day it *would* fall forward, that I'd hear that crash of glassware again. The thing was, I knew it was a completely unfounded fear with the new place. I knew that wouldn't have been an issue in such an updated and sturdy kitchen. However, it didn't matter; my mind was trained for that reaction. Even though I knew logically that my dishwasher was reliable, I couldn't shake the occasional fear of it falling forward again.

Just because the thing that broke your trust in the first place is gone from your life, doesn't mean that the fear doesn't still live inside your head. That's the basis of residual trauma. Sure, having a shaky and untrustworthy dishwasher isn't a big issue. It's nothing that's going to keep you up at night. However, what about an untrustworthy partner? What about living with someone for years who made you feel like you had to walk on eggshells?

Once you get out of a relationship that has broken your trust or caused you extreme emotional stress, it takes a lot of personal time before you are able to feel safe again. This is because broken trust is the highest form of betrayal. You are going to be nervous about trusting again, even once you have healed. Even though you have moved forward, those trust issues are still going to be on your mind from time to time.

To make this book one of the most accurate and interactive publications that I possibly could, I reached out to some of my readers with questions on some of the issues we have all faced in the dating world. I wanted to know the main concerns that they had when they first started putting themselves out there in their search for love.

The responses were overwhelmingly about trust: "How can I trust if she's going to cheat or not?" "How can I trust she's an honest woman, if her intentions are pure?" or, "What if I fall for her and she cheats on me?"

Ouch. Okay, first things first: you've been hurt. It genuinely breaks my heart to see so many of going through this. You didn't start out with trust issues, none of us did. Before all this, once upon a time, you opened up to a partner and loved freely. You have to find a way to regain that mindset with someone new, no matter how heavy your baggage is. You *need* to open up again.

We all have someone who wrenched our heart out and crushed it, someone who left us guarded and cautious. Someone who stripped us of feeling loved and left us feeling abandoned in a relationship. Once that happens, we are at risk of speaking that scenario into existence and living it again.

It is important to understand that this lesson was crucial and it was meant to be learned, but it shouldn't be a negative one. Instead, consider it a failure that you can build on and use as a strength. It is our responsibility as human beings to seek help for our previous traumas and do our best to not project them onto a new relationship. If not, we will continue that destructive path and ruin what could potentially be a new, loving, and healthy relationship.

Yes, I'm telling you to *"Get over it."*

Your future partner should absolutely be someone you can be honest and open with, *but they are not responsible for healing you from your past.* That is your mission. Before finding the love of your life, you have to forgive yourself for your past mistakes and trust that you've learned from them. I know it's not typical for most men to seek out therapy or counseling, but trust me, self-care is the manliest thing you can do. I have not yet met a woman who looks down on a man who cares about his mental health and proactively chooses to maintain it. A man that takes care of his body *and* his mind? That's sexy. It's a new generation, people, and we're focusing on mental stability and self-care. (Feel free to read that again, and again, and again!)

My second thought imme-diately goes to the reasons *why* people cheat or have trust issues in relationships. It has been studied over and over again, and consistently found that the main reason people cheat is because they are missing some-thing. They feel unloved, unappreciated, or unaccepted by their partner. Sure, this is true in a lot of situations, but it can also be a complete crock-of-shit.

Erase from your mind the stigma that cheating is one-sided. Instead, start to think of it like this: the person who cheats is not always the villain, and the person who was cheated on is not always the victim. There is such a wide range of reasons that people give as to why they cheated, but here's the big secret: they fucking *wanted* to cheat.

It doesn't mean that they didn't love you, or you didn't love them. So if you were the "cheater" or the "cheatee" in your last relationship, it doesn't matter. You can still have a trusting, meaningful relationship if you work towards it. It all starts with forgiving the person who did the deed, even if that person is yourself, and understanding why it happened. Most importantly, remember to take control of the narrative and accept it for what it is.

One day you'll move on to someone new.

You'll have a sturdy, reliable, new dishwasher. And you know what? You're still going to have doubts about your partner. Even if there is no reason for it. When this happens, there are two things that need to go down: first of all, you have to be strong enough to realize that you are living through anxiety caused by past traumas. Secondly, your partner has to be strong and understanding enough to accept your past without taking any of it personally.

This is why healing your traumas is the most important factor in establishing a new relationship. Yes, your partner should be there for you and reassure you when you have doubts. They can also love you and support you through your hard times, but it isn't their job to heal you. You will burn out any friendship or relationship very quickly if you rely on them as a therapist instead of just, you know, getting an actual therapist.

With that being said, there are people out there who can't

help themselves: they are habitual cheaters. You can't control that trait in a person; that's an issue they have to deal with. Whether it has to do with a lack of respect and control, or it could be linked to their traumatic childhood. Either way, they have to heal that part of them on their own. Just please understand when a situation like this happens to you: *it's not your fault.* Some people are not made for monogamy. There are many books on polygamy that explains how polygamous relationships differ vastly from monogamous love. It's a highly respected, trust-based, sustainable relationship in its own right, but I won't be including any chapters on that here as it's way too vast of a topic to cover in a monogamy-based dating book.

However, aside from poly-amorous relationships, practicing honesty and openness in the beginning will create a foundation of friendship and trust that will likely prevent a betrayal from happening. You would never cheat your best friend out of something that would better their future. You would never betray your siblings or your family, right? Think of your partner as that: your close friend and family. There is an incredibly strong foundation of trust that goes with that title.

Some words of wisdom my Nana once gave me have stuck with me since childhood. She said, "A cheater is a cheater, you either love 'em or you leave 'em."

Your concern with trust in a developing relationship is valid. Do you want to develop a trusting and honest relationship with your dream woman? If so, you're going to have to take a leap of faith on each other. You've been cheated on, you've been lied to, and you have trust issues. I guarantee that is going to be something you have in common with your Bunny. You have to trust each other; that's part of developing a solid friendship first. If you can work on healing your insecurities while understanding that she deserves patience with hers as well, then you're off to a fantastic start.

CHAPTER 2

Establishing Friendship

Think of some of the things only your closest friend knows about you: from childhood memories to embarrassing nights out, I'm sure there are a lot of things you wouldn't want to reveal to a woman you want to be intimate with.

However, this is actually the level of friendship you should strive to have with your Bunny.

Of course, close friendships do not start out with sharing your deepest, darkest secrets (that would be... awkward). It usually starts out with you both bonding over a shared interest, like a sport or a game or a favorite tv series. Most of your closest friends you probably met through a place or hobby that you both liked or attended.

Having a shared interest or hobby always brings people closer together. That's why camping or traveling with your family or closest friends is so fun; it's the time spent laughing and bonding that provides positive, lasting memories.

A woman will always remember the way you make her

feel, and that is why starting off with a solid, fun, and adventurous friendship is so important.

If you can keep her laughing, then she will keep you around. It's not always the tallest, most fit guy in the room who gets the girl. A real woman knows that looks won't last, but the feelings will. Although the male model in the center of the room is going to get some glances, a woman is going to end up remembering the person who made her laugh the most or feel the best about herself.

Trust me on this one, there have been plenty of times my girls and I refer to some guy as "What's-his-name" the next day, but the guy who spent time getting to know us and making us laugh was saved in our contacts under his real name. That's because showing interest makes her feel appreciated, and appreciation makes the heart grow fonder.

A lot of women have said that a strong sense of humor is crucial when they're looking for a partner. This makes a lot of sense because laughing makes you feel great! However, what these women fail to realize is that they're actually looking for a partner with a similar sense of humor to their own.

For example, my best friend and I laugh at each other's jokes all day. It's a non-stop smile fest when we hang out, and it's one of the reasons she's my closest friend. We have trust, respect, and tons of laughter!

If I compare the friendship I have with her to a failed relationship of mine in the past, I realize that we didn't share the same sense of humor at all. In fact, he almost never laughed or did anything to make me laugh either. I would jokingly blurt out "come on, that was funny!" After I said a joke or did something I perceived as funny, but he did not respond to it. It ultimately gave me the impression that he didn't like me, and I felt judged or looked down upon. At the very least, I felt like he was bored with me.

If you are able to get those endorphins running while making her laugh, then that will make her feel more comfortable with you. Making her feel at ease is a great first step to her wanting to spend more time with you.

Having fun together is a huge cornerstone to a woman, and any man who can make her laugh and feel comfortable around is a man she would want to consistency spend time with.

And speaking of hanging out on a consistent basis, do yourself a favor and stop with any of those childish "make her wait" games. Prioritize her schedule and plan in advance, if you can! It shows interest in her and respect for her time.

Think about it, would you play the three-day waiting game with your closest friend to see if it makes him want to hang out you more, or be honest about when you are free to hang out? Do you like it when people play games like that with you? Hell no! You'd prioritize your time with your friends, because you enjoy spending time with them. The same thing applies to building a deep and strong relationship with your Bunny. It also shows respect for her time when you pre-plan out some adventures or fun hangouts with her. So, ditch the old idea that whichever one of you cares the least is the one who gets hurt the least, because genuinely caring is the *real* deal.

Doing something that you both like definitely makes the date feel less awkward and more fun! Plus, she'll be genuinely looking forward to spending that time with you. It also shows that you took the initiative to find out what she likes, which shows that you really listen to her when she expresses interest in something. She gets to do something she enjoys doing, with someone who listens when she talks about her life, and who took the initiative to set it up? That's a happy, positive feeling that she'll remember.

Couples who have been married for a long time agree that the secret to a long-lasting relationship is a strong friendship. Just think of how long your friendships have lasted versus your longest relationship. Another reason these relationships last is because good friend-ships have a strong foundation of respect. When you respect someone, you respond to their texts quickly and you value their time. Therefore, developing a strong, deep friendship is one of the best guides to building a love that will last. Plus, spending all that time with your clos-est friend is an all-around win!

CHAPTER 3

Be Your Best Self

You've probably heard that women want you to "Just be yourself" when you're heading out on those first few hang-outs. Well, this may be confusing, but not technically. Always be your genuine self, *respectfully*. There's a level of being open that definitely qualifies as "too open" for the first date. That leave-the-bathroom-door-wide-open-as-you-poop level of honesty and comfort comes with time. In the beginning you want her to feel respected, and comfortable. Just as a side-note, for some women, that level of openness will always be considered "not-okay" or disrespectful, so listen to her cues when it comes to things like that.

What women really mean when we say "be yourself" is we want to get to know you. The *real* you. The passionate gamer who is nationally ranked on Call of Duty, the band nerd who loves his trumpet so much it's always out on the dresser, the artist who spends all of his spare time researching his craft, and even the *Star Wars* fan that brings his replica lightsaber to work. That is the "you" we want to know.

Seeing a man with a passion is the sexiest thing for a woman. I want to see you in your element, doing what you love, with genuine and raw excitement. It's the best way to get to know you. Women love to see you open up, and this is the coolest way to show your Bunny what you love. It shows her you can have comradery with your friends and work on a team, and it also shows off your depth and emotion. We *love* that stuff.

Think about how happy you are when you're doing something you love. Are you relaxed? Happy? Comfortable? That is exactly how a woman wants you to be around her. It makes her feel like she's your teammate, your best friend. It opens up a level of trust and makes her feel like she's a part of your squad. It gives her a genuine feeling of value and priority. It's also the best way for her to know you're being your honest and genuine self around her.

What about when you're having a bad week, or a bad year even? Sometimes we aren't always the luckiest in life and things aren't perfect. What do you do when you really want to show her the best version of yourself, but you just can't?

Being your best self isn't a financial or monetary state of being. Your *best* self is a state of mind. You can be down in the dumps or down on your luck and still have a positive mindset. This aligns with the first chapter about healing yourself, but on a slightly different level. If all you're ever projecting is positivity, not only is it fake, but it's not realistic. We all have those moments where we are rebuilding our life. Even recovering addicts have a full program of steps that require them to be on their own. You have to get your shit together before you can start looking for a partner.

Just because you don't love where you are in life, does not mean you are not worthy of love.

There are obviously times in our lives where we have to resort to a less-than-ideal version of ourselves. You know, those times when someone loses their job, their drive, or their motivation and they have to move back in with their parents or friends.

That's okay.

Remember that two of the most important steps in a long term and loving relationship are honesty and communication. Being honest about where you are in your life, even if it's not an ideal place in your mind, is still admirable.

Be passionate about moving forward with your plans, your life, and your passions. Be honest about achieving your *best* self and stick with it.

It's okay to fall down but staying in that place of failure and resentment isn't the best version of yourself. It's certainly not going to keep the Bunny of your dreams around if she doesn't see you getting back up again and working towards the things that make you happy to be who you are.

Establishing yourself as someone you aren't will eventually leave you with growing resentment. You cannot fake those passions and interests for long, and you will always be trapped into that persona for as long as you are together. It's stressful, right?

Getting to know you more means she's giving you a chance

to show her you are worth trusting as a companion. Putting your fake foot forward is misleading. Dating is meant to be a fun way to get to know each other, so keep it fun! One of my favorite sayings is "Be you and be cool with it." Don't try to impress her, just be your best self.

CHAPTER 4

How Fast is Too Fast?

First of all, as exciting as things are when you start consistently hanging out, remember that moving too quickly can come off as aggressive and annoying. This is especially true if you're both not on the same level emotionally or mentally. Make sure you respect her space and trust your gut if you feel like you're going to get rejected. Being too pushy can come off as creepy or ill-intentioned and she can shut you down before she gives you a fair chance.

Think of relationships like this analogy: when you're hungry, you can opt for a few different types of meals. The quickest is fast food, and the longest is cooking a meal at home from scratch. The fast food will always fill you up initially, but after the hunger subsides, you're left feeling regretful. The home cooked meal, however, will take longer but will taste better and it will also make your body feel better, too.

Another problem with moving too quickly is risking being overly vulnerable. Trust doesn't come naturally; it's built over time. So many people are hurt from previous relationships and a long pattern of disappointments. She's likely in the same boat as you are and needs things to move slowly so you can both earn each other's trust. There is strength in being open and vulnerable with someone you care about.

It's no secret that I've been through this more than once. My first marriage was the poster child on how-not-to-love. We started out fast, and we decided to move in together after the first date. We had no clue who we were. I remember idealizing him so much that I completely changed who I was just so I could impress him. Eventually, he popped the question. We then got married and had our son, all in very quick succession.

Since the affection we had for each other was based on a false narrative that I had created in order to "bag" him, there was not a solid base of friendship or trust. He would see little glimpses of what I was truly passionate about, but they did not fit his idea of our future. Eventually, the fighting and resentment became too heavy of a burden.

We had zero trust, which led to more fights, and these fights added more pressure to the façade we put on for our families. It became difficult to uphold a perfect image, and eventually it all shattered. I did my best to be the person I thought he wanted instead of just being honest and being myself.

No honesty = no trust.

I then began projecting my own dishonesty onto him, which in return led to him not trusting me. I knew I had to get out of the lie that we had been living in. I nuked that relationship and walked away from the explosion like a protagonist in an action movie.

Now that I am in a healthy and loving relationship, I see what a difference it makes when you are patient. There's a much stronger bond when you take your time. With this new relationship, we already had an established friendship for a few years, so there was already a foundation of trust. Naturally, we had a lot in common, and I've always felt safe around him because he never hit on me or did anything that could be interpreted as "creepy." The first time we hung out alone at my place, we played a card game and drank some whisky. I fell asleep on the couch, he tucked me in, and cleaned up the card game. He also left me a hand-written note that said, "Thank you for the most amazing night of my life."

It was a sweet and romantic gesture that did not come off too pushy or aggressive. It made me realize he wanted to spend more time with me without him even asking yet. Most importantly, it left me in charge of the decision on whether or not I wanted to get to know him more.

So how fast is too fast?

You know that buddy of yours who falls in love with every girl he goes on a first date with? You can usually tell what he did wrong: obsessing over her without getting to know her first. Moving forward at light speed rarely works out because real love takes time.

How fast things move romantically should ultimately be up to her, but you can help by putting the ball in her court.

This is where the saying "Patience is a virtue" comes in.

I know, it's the most cliché saying in the world, but it's common for a reason. With that being said, I know it takes a lot of effort to keep yourself from jumping in with both feet at the first sign of those warm fuzzy feelings. Everything in today's society is instant, while relationships still take time. That's why it's so hard! "I want her, and I want her to want me, and I need to find out how to make this work *right now*" but trust me, you cannot rush a lasting relationship!

Developing a strong bond of trust takes time, and it starts with a leap of faith. My partner took a leap of faith on me, and I reciprocated that. I could genuinely see that effort. That's what real love is all about, and that's the first step to creating a bond that will last.

CHAPTER 5

Love Language and Body Language.

Figure out her love language. It's not something you should just ask but not try to understand either.

Everyone gives and receives love differently. If receiving gifts is not one of your love languages, then you might not understand what your partner means when she admits "Well, I find that receiving tangible gifts makes me happy." Or if acts of service is not a love language you are familiar with, then you might not understand what your partner means when she says "If I write love notes and they aren't reciprocated, I'll feel bad." It can sound selfish to just blurt out what your love language is randomly, so it is best to have this conversation early. You or your partner might discover that you both have more than one love language, and that is where things can get a bit complicated.

It's not an easy task but understanding the difference between how you perceive love and how she perceives love is important. If one person shows love with gifts and flowers, and

the other with physical affection or time spent together,
then both efforts will come up
short. The end result will be one
or both of you will start to feel
unloved, which would lead to a
resentful relationship.

Note that you don't have to
speak the same love language
as your Bunny, but you do have
to put in the effort to learn her
love language. You also have to
trust that she is doing the same
for you. Ultimately, learning
each other's love languages is a
form of communication as well.

The Five Love Languages
(And an added bonus):

1. Quality Time
    As a love language, qual-
    ity time is a no-brainer.

You are either someone who values it highly , or you have been in a relationship where it was highly valued. Quality time is a very common and highly noticeable love language. Ask yourself this:

Do you prefer to stay in and spend time together? Does a good date consist of strong eye contact during conversations where you both talk about your day, hopes, and dreams? Maybe you prefer cooking a meal together in the kitchen as opposed to going to a fancy restaurant?

These are just a few examples of valuing quality time and using it as a way you show affection. The more you love someone, the more time you would want to spend with them.

This is exactly how someone whose main love language is "Quality Time" perceives love.

2. Receiving Gifts
   This love language often falls under scrutiny because most people think

it's all about material-ism and not about the thoughts and emotions behind the gift. Someone who values gifts as a form of affection is not nec-essarily materialistic or shallow, as the language might imply.

In fact, most people whose main love lan-guage is receiving gifts are extremely gener-ous. They show affec-tion by giving gifts, as well as receiving them. Someone with this love language is highly likely to surprise you with lit-tle things that remind them of you throughout their day, such as gifts, flowers, or cards.

In return, they also highly value the same thoughtfulness from their partners. A surprise note on the fridge, their favorite dessert after they've had a long day, or a small gift that lets them know you were thinking about them would mean the world to someone whose primary love language is receiving gifts.

3. Physical Touch
This particular love language is not just about

sex. All love languages aside, a healthy and deep relationship will always have great sex as one of its cornerstones.

No, this particular love language is referring to actual, daily physical touch. Holding hands, loving embraces, even just touching their shoulder as you walk past them when you're both busy. Someone who values physical touch and perceives love this way will be a snuggler, cuddle bug, and a PDA kind of person.

They can come across as needy because it is in their nature to want to touch, kiss, hug, and hold hands. However, this is how they show love; therefore, reciprocating these touches is how they would feel loved by their partners.

4. Words of Affirmation
   This is another one of the love languages that can come across as needy, or even insecure. Words of affirmation can be as simple as putting your arm around someone and announcing, "Hey, I like this person!" Some

people simply need to assure that you love them through spoken words.

Words of affirmation can be anything from a "Hey, I appreciate you," or "I love you so much" on a regular basis. This might not mean a lot to you or seem important at all, especially if this isn't a love language that you both share; however, it would mean the world to someone whose primary love language is words of affirmation.

Someone who needs words of affirmation

throughout their day are simply looking for you to cheer them, encourage them, and remind them that they are loved. In return, they will also be just as vocal for you.

5. Acts of Service
This love language can be traced back to religious and biblical upbringings. More than likely, someone who grew up being taught that worship and love were shown through service is the same person who will grow up doing the same. For example, a common

service of love is your partner doing the dishes after you cook. For them, it's seen as a form of appreciation for the delicious meal.

Those whose primary love language is acts of service would appreciate you opening the door for them, picking up groceries or running an errand you know they have been dreading. Even something as simple as massaging their feet after a long day at work will not go unnoticed.

To them, it's a selfless act of love and the only intent they have is to make your life easier and less stressful. On the other hand, if you aren't someone who shows affection through acts like these, they can feel awkward to you. It can cause a rift in your relationship if you refuse acts of service from a person who uses that as a main way to show their love for you. They can feel rejected, left out and unwanted. So understanding that this is their love language can help you receive their love as well as help you make them feel loved in return.

6. Bonus: <u>Distance</u>
This love language is one that is one that I've created myself, and I feel that it's an important one to add. Technically, giving your partner space can go under "Acts of Service." However, I feel like this is its own separate language of love.

For some people, being left alone is the highest form of love you can give them. Right now, we live in a world where we are flooded with information and contact every single second of the day. From social media, to working from our phones and computers, to answering text messages, and a barrage of marketing everywhere we turn. Because of that, a lot of people suffer from depression and anxiety. You're either an introvert or an extrovert, and thanks to the way the world works these days, most people are leaning towards the introvert side.

So, no matter her love language, some days your Bunny may just need her space. Even giving space in your own home by staying in another room and reading a book while she gets work done or drinks her cup of coffee or glass of wine. Understanding and accepting that strong relationships require space, is a love language all on its own.

There are a lot of ways to give and receive love, and this is why communication is key in any relationship. Understanding how you give and receive love is important for the foundation of the relationship. Just like personality types, there is no one-size-fits-all love language. Remember, you can have a main love language, but still have attributes of another one.

That's the beautiful thing about these separate and different languages: the combinations are just as diverse as we are. You can share a second or third love language with your Bunny but have polar opposite primary love languages, and that's okay! As long as you communicate what makes you feel loved, your partner should respect and reciprocate it.

CHAPTER 6

Don't Be An Asshole.

You have heard women from all walks of life agree on one thing: All men are assholes.

But not you, right? I hope not!

Let's look at how to recognize what kind of asshole you might be perceived as, and how to change that perception.

Here are a few examples of notorious asshole behavior that

you might not have known you were exhibiting:

The Rich:

Bragging/cocky behavior can come across as demeaning. All you're doing is talking about yourself and while you think you're providing her with reasons to go on a second date, you're actually pushing her away. She doesn't want to hear about your designer taste or expensive toys, she wants to hear about you. Humility will go a long way. Bragging about your income or your possessions only makes you look like you have nothing substantial to offer her emotionally. Remember, most of the love languages are based on how you give and receive love. Even those whose primary love language is receiving gifts are not impressed only by the material objects. They view gifts as a sign of love because of the thought that was put behind them, not because of the price tag.

The Entitled:

Being rude to wait staff or the cab driver will paint you as a pretentious jerk. Even if you're respectful to her, but disrespectful to everyone else, you might as well consider yourself blocked. It also shows her that you have a complete disregard for people who you deemed non-beneficial. It gives you the appearance of someone who uses people to their advantage, her included.

"Why is he being respectful to me but not to the driver or the maintenance staff?" She will wonder if it is because she has something you want, and those other people don't. It makes you look shallow and entitled, and above all, untrustworthy. Using some humility and genuine compassion with strangers on the street is impressive to a woman who values those qualities. Oh, and using your manners doesn't hurt either. Trust me, it's extremely sexy when a man smiles and says "thank you ma'am" to a stranger.

The Angry:

Are you known for your road rage? Do you slam your laptop shut when it freezes? Have you ever punched a hole in a wall because you dropped a canister of shaving cream on your toe? (No lie, my ex actually did that once).

In case you didn't know, one of the biggest turn-offs is someone with an unchecked anger problem. Not only is it a red flag for potential future arguments, but it's terrifying. Handle tense situations with a relaxed demeanor, which means have some chill factor, and be a safe driver. Show her you can stay cool under pressure and she'll feel more relaxed about the hangout. It also is a sign of compassion and empathy towards other people.

Don't get me wrong, it's completely normal to get angry about things. Anger is a natural human emotion. It's your reaction to anger that defines who you are as a person. So, don't be *that* asshole.

The "My Ex is Crazy":

Come on, is that really what she wants to talk about? You're not the first man to try to make himself look better by painting his ex as the villain, but here's something you may not know: flaunting problems with your last break up is only going to make her wonder what *you* did to make her that way.

Yes, that's right, we always consider the ex's perspective. Each and every one of us have been called crazy (among other things) and we all have each other's backs. Do yourself a favor and skip the pity party about your last break up.

Of course, we know that there are women out there who are *truly* deserving of that "Psycho" title. Trust me, we all have met them, we know them personally, and we have probably tried to talk them out of their bat-shit behavior at one point or another.

The point is, your Bunny doesn't want to hear the drama.

Stick to something more positive and it will make hanging out with you a more positive (and less asshole-ish) experience.

The Busy:

Are you the guy who just has to have your phone in hand the whole time you're out? You're that successful, popular, or busy, right? Either your business, your personal life, or your social media keeps poppin' off and you think it makes you look desirable because you're so desired by everyone else? Nope. Even if you're genuinely overwhelmed by work and can't possibly give her the time of day, this isn't a good look.

The message you're sending to your Bunny is that you don't

have time for her. You don't even have the attention span to look her in the eyes while she talks about things that are important to her. You are completely unavailable, despite being right there in front of her. In all honesty, in today's world this is a very easy mistake to make. Sometimes you are just waiting on that important email or text, and if that's the case, just pre-warn her. Yep, it's another instance where communication is key! But if you're just one of those assholes who prioritizes their social media presence or their work over personal time spent with her, your Bunny is going to be long gone by the time you look up.

This was actually the beginning of the downfall in one of my previous relationships: I felt like my husband was married to his job and his clients, not to me. My wants or desires or even my schedule didn't matter to him because he was always buried in his phone or computer, always *so busy*. His phone was more important to him than I was.

What did I do to pass the time while he was checking his phone? I'd get lost in mine as well. Eventually we didn't spend any quality time together and instead, we'd spend most of it staring at a screen. I started finding other people to call or talk to who would actually made me feel like they valued my conversation. It's a slow killer, but a relationship killer nonetheless. Put your phone away, and you won't look like a busy asshole.

The Over-Opinionated:

As I have said before, being passionate about a hobby or subject is an extremely sexy quality. That passion crosses the line into an asshole-esque quality once you start forcing those beliefs on your Bunny. It can be anything from politics to dietary habits.

There's a well-meaning behind it, of course, but you also have to remember that she's a woman who has formed her own opinions and trusts them. To completely negate or undermine her beliefs simply because they are not what you've studied or practiced is demeaning. Over time, it can cause tension in the relationship. If you both differ on certain nutritional habits or religious beliefs or even a phone brand, just remember to respect her opinions. Otherwise, she'll think you're just a controlling asshole.

The Broke:

Before you start thinking this is all about money, it's not. This is more about responsibility, safety nets, and financial sustainability. Having a steady income and being able to manage your money is crucial. If you can't afford a fancy dinner date, then don't choose to go on one!

Double check that you have your wallet before inviting her out for something, and don't choose an option that's going to break your bank. An independent woman loves being able to pick up the tab, but it's even sexier when you acknowledge she can do so but you still choose to treat her.

If you can't take her out, do something free that you'll both enjoy. However, if you can't afford the date, do not expect her to pay for it. Also, if you "forget your wallet" at home, you can probably go ahead and forget her number too while you're at it.

Having a lack of independence is a huge turn-off and

a lack of motivation or drive seems to go hand-in-hand with that. No one wants to spend their life arguing over finances. In fact, statistically speaking, couples argue the most about financial stresses.

Look, almost everyone starts out with nothing. You do not have to own your own business or fly private charters in order to impress her. However, if you aren't smart with your money and have no plan to be independently sustainable in the future, then she'll assume you're just a broke asshole.

The Lying:

Okay fellas, this is the big one. Honesty is always the absolute best policy. What is something you'd potentially lie about? Income, status, past behaviors, women you've slept with? Maybe you know that there is something in your past that is a deal-breaker for her, and you don't want to risk offending her or losing her. I'll say this for you loud and clear: no matter what it is, DON'T LIE TO HER.

Listen up, if you really want to be with this woman, you have to come out with it. We're like FBI agents: we're going to find out anyways and it would be better if we found out from you … Starting out the relationship on a lie decimates all future trust. Come on, that's one of the most important cornerstones of a strong relationship and you're going to blow it right off the bat with a lie?

I'll never forget when I was just starting out my first serious relationship in my twenties. I had so much fun with this person and so much in common with him, but there was one downfall. My closest friend at the time found an old, separate social media account that listed him as "married." I confronted him about it in the most awkward way possible, because how else do you ask the person you're falling for if they're holding back a giant omission?

"Hey, um, are you... married?" His face turned red and he opened up to me that he was actually in the midst of a separation and divorce. I appreciated his honesty once I asked about it, but it should have been the first thing on the table when we started dating.

Being honest is the sexiest thing you can be, even if it initially sucks to have to come clean. She will respect you in the long run for communicating with her openly. Plus, it develops a strong sense of trust, it shows your humility, and makes you look like an all-around good guy instead of a lying asshole.

The Controlling:

This one goes back to chapter one's subject on healing your

traumas. If you feel the need to dictate where your woman works, what she eats, who she hangs out with, or how she is overall perceived by people around you… then you are going to lose her faster than the door can slam shut on her way out.

Part of loving someone is accepting them for every aspect of their life. There is a difference between encouraging someone to be the best version of themselves and forcing it on them. It's blatantly obvious when you aren't proud of your Bunny for her being herself. Let's say your ideal woman is someone with a passion for fitness and veggies, but you fall for the woman who loves pizza and sweets instead. Encouraging her to join you at the gym because you want to include her in your hobby is great! However, going through her pantry and throwing away all of her favorite foods is not so great.

For example, I remember bluntly having to ask someone I dated to be proud of my modeling accomplishments. Magazine covers, calendars, features, anything that I was proud of I wanted him to be proud of too! Instead, I had to beg him to share the good news, or I would resort to sharing the news myself. As it turns out, no one in his family was supportive of it either. As our relationship developed, I realized that I was looked down on for my career choice and I could tell he was nervous to even talk about it outside of our home. It made me not want to be proud of it, too.

Basically, there is a balance between loving someone and trying to change them into a version you'd love more. That is the difference between a loving partner and the controlling asshole.

So, are you an asshole?

Also, understand that a lot of these behaviors are characterized as emotionally abusive and are red flags. Of course, that can go both ways. If your Bunny exhibits these behaviors, then she needs time to heal from her traumas before she's ready for her forever relationship.

A lot of times these behaviors are embedded in us from

our upbringing or a toxic parent, or even the expectations of past relationships. That is why the very first chapter of this book is about healing your traumas: sometimes what comes natural to you is actually a toxic learned behavior from your past. As humans, we are designed to protect ourselves, which is where toxic behavior and PTSD comes from. I always, always suggest seeking professional help if you find that you or someone you've been in love with has exhibited these qualities. Healing yourself is the most un-asshole thing you can do, and it's an incredibly emotionally mature decision that will strengthen both you and your relationships, whether they are romantic or not.

So don't be an asshole, be a healed and emotionally mature person who was formerly known as an asshole.

CHAPTER 7

Perfection is Subjective

I'm going to come right out and say it: Stop giving a fuck about how your relationship is perceived by other people because years from now it's not going to matter how many likes your #couplesgoals post got on social media.

"You guys are such a beautiful couple." "Wow you look so good together!" "Oh that house you both live in is gorgeous," etc.

These compliments are not only a reflection of how you are perceived. Instead, they actually show the insecurities of the person who is complimenting you. Aka, they want what you have and idealize how their future success should look simply based on photos and social media posts about your life.

Instead, try to live your life without feeling the need to boast about it to the world. How much happier would you be if you were solely focused on building strong cornerstones of love and friendship internally instead of just talking about how happy you are to everyone else?

Like my favorite mogul from the 305, Pitbull, said: "Don't talk about it, *BE* about it." Build love and let it shine through your actions, not your posts.

I'll never forget one of my worst wedding anniversaries.

At the time I was a bartender at a sports bar. On Thursdays, we had a $1 beer special. This Thursday in particular, I had requested work off. I had asked my mother-in-law to watch our infant son, so my husband and I could celebrate together.

Unfortunately, the night before we had an argument over who-knows-what, and he wasn't speaking to me. This was actually a common reoccurrence. After an argument, we would go through a day or so of awkward, silent non-interaction. I wasn't aware at the time, but this is one of the many forms of emotional abuse he exhibited. He scheduled extra clients at work, and I tried to pick up a shift so we wouldn't have to see each other. As it turns out, we were over staffed that night and no one would let me pick up a shift. I decided to sit at the bar instead of going home to a husband who was giving me the silent treatment. All day long he had not responded to a single text message I had sent, picked up any of my phone calls, or even wished me a happy anniversary.

There I was, alone at the bar on "dollar-beer-night." I was scrolling through social media in an attempt to get my mind off of things and what did I see? A post on his page, that I was tagged in.

It read something like "Happy anniversary to my loving, caring, supermom wife. I'm so blessed to have you in my life, you are my everything, I love you. Here's to many more years of love and growth... blah blah blah." The post has long since been taken down, but it was a long paragraph of sappy, fake bullshit.

This wasn't the first time something like that had happened and it wouldn't be the last. It was all part of the show: everyone had to think we were perfect, when in reality we were empty on the inside. I even had a co-worker the next day come to me and praise our relationship. She said, "I read what your hubby wrote about you! You are the most adorable couple I have ever seen! One day, I hope to find a love like yours. You are so lucky!"

To her surprise, I started laughing. "Girl, I spent last night right here at the bar. Alone. Don't believe everything you see on the internet."

You never know what someone's personal life is like because only the positive, happy posts on social media get any attention. If you put out the truth about your life, it's often shunned as negativity and gets called out for being overly dramatic. People pick and choose how they want to be perceived. My last relationship was forced into the narcissistic perception of perfection. He never even so much as spoke to his siblings or his friends about our relationship, so when I left to pursue my own happiness, the only people who weren't surprised were my close family and friends. No one on his side had a clue we were so miserable.

There's also a red flag here that you might be involved with a narcissist if the only thing they care about is the outward perception of your relationship. Narcissistic personality disorder is when a person has an inflated sense of self-importance. However, although we all swear that we know that one person who fits that diagnosis, there are fewer than 200,000 cases a year, so I wouldn't bet on it. Social media gets to a lot of people but it doesn't mean that they need to be medicated. Just balance it out with some reality every once in a while.

Work on your relationship from the inside-out, with humility and respect. Don't compare yourself to the picture-perfect couples on the internet. That's their life, not yours. Happiness only comes from within yourself, so don't worry about anyone else and focus on your growth. You'll quickly stop caring about what "perfection" looks like when you feel it from the inside.

Do you want everyone to think you're happy, or do you *really* want to be happy?

CHAPTER 8

Understanding the "Creep" Factor

There are so many different ways to define "creepy" that the best I can do for you, instead of defining it, is explain to you *why* women perceive men as creepy. This is pretty much our brain's way of protecting ourselves. It goes hand in hand with what we call a woman's intuition, our basic instincts of survival.

If you even need to ask why women are intimidated or guarded when they meet a man for the first time, it's first and foremost because of the sheer physical factor. Your body is basically a weapon compared to ours, so much so that most women carry a weapon with them when they walk alone just to even the playing field. Unfortunately, women are statistically at a greater risk for sexual assault than men. It's not just us watching too much *Law & Order SVU* and being paranoid, it's a fact. So, keeping that in mind, let's go back to why a woman might think a man is "creepy."

Of course, we all go through an awkward phase when we're

new to dating or just haven't gotten out of the house to socialize with new people in a while. That's fine! There's a fine line between being awkward and being a creep.

For women, anyone being described as a "creep" is basically our way of saying, "I don't know that person very well but I feel like they could potentially harm me." This are based on the imbalance of power between the sexes. Understanding this imbalance and having empathy for it is important, especially when you're approaching a woman you see potential with. Our deepest concerns when interacting with you for the first time are wildly different than yours.

For a man, a bad date would end in some sort of embarrassing sexual humiliation.

For a woman, a bad date can end up with us being physically harmed, sexually assaulted, abducted, or murdered. Most of us women are statistically risking our lives by agreeing to meet up with you for a drink, so have a little empathy and respect her boundaries from the beginning. Trust me, we can tell the difference.

What does a creepy date look like for a female? Well, here's a little bit of perspective for you. Back when I was living in Los Angeles, I was notoriously single and happy with it. I rarely went on dates and I worked all the time. Naturally, the only dating scene I was in at the time was online, and I didn't trust anyone I didn't know personally.

One evening my curiosity got the best of me. I had been talking on the phone with this guy for a few nights and I decided to meet him. I drove separately, as per my rules, but things were going well, and I felt comfortable enough to get in the car with this person and head to the next bar.

On our way there, despite the light and friendly conversation, I couldn't help but notice that we were headed in the opposite direction of the bars. In fact, I noticed we were headed towards a canyon that I hiked frequently, and I knew that once we got there, my phone would lose service.

I panicked. I tried to calmly ask him where he was headed, and when he lied and said we were headed to the bar, but I called him out on it.

"This is the way to the canyon. Look, I have my GPS up, we're going in the opposite direction." He didn't budge. He kept silent. I called my roommates and put them on speaker phone while I kept my GPS open. I told them where I was, where he was driving, and described his vehicle. Right as my phone was about to cut out, they said "We're on our way, we've called the cops, we're getting to you as fast as we can."

He slammed on the brakes, angrily told me to get out of the car, and I obliged. I don't think I could have jumped out any faster if the damn thing was on fire. I started walking back down the hill towards the entryway to the canyon when my roommates pulled up, spotted me in their headlights, and pulled over to rescue me.

This was a normal, nice guy who I thought had no intention of hurting me. Yes, that was an extreme circumstance. I know the chances of this happening to me again are pretty low, considering I'm a paranoid bucketo-crazy now, but scenarios like this happen all the time.

So that girl that you're interested in and want to meet up with for your first date? There's a big chance that she's had something creepy happen to her. The basics of discerning creep factor is based on how safe she feels.

So what is the opposite of "creepy" and how do you achieve it?

For us, the word women use for a guy we don't find creepy is "safe." I've used it to define many of my past relationships or even just friendships I have with men. I've reassured my family of my safety by saying, "I'm staying at so-and-so's house when I land. Don't worry, he's harmless."

That proves right away that "creep" is a term we use when we feel like there is a potential for danger with that particular person. In order to be labeled as someone we feel "safe" around, just remember that we're out to protect ourselves from being another statistic. I'm not saying you have to approach us like fragile, scared little bunnies. You should, however, be aware of signals that she's uncomfortable, and give her some space. Trust me, she'll notice, and appreciate it.

Basically, is what you're doing going to make her feel safe?

CHAPTER 9

Building a Strong Relationship and Keeping It!

I've mentioned a lot about certain cornerstones of a relationship, so now let's expand on them. A cornerstone in a building is the ceremonial first block laid to the foundation of the building. In a relationship, however, you need more than just that one block to build upon.

A foundation is not made up of just one big important thing, but a system of smaller important qualities and actions that are woven together. More like the nerves in a spine rather than one singular brick. In order to have a strong and healthy spine, you have to make sure all of your discs, nerves, and vertebrae are properly aligned.

So, instead of focusing on a few large cornerstones, let's focus on a healthy back bone. Here are some of the most important aspects to form and keep a long-lasting love.

Trust:

One of the more commonly known aspects of a healthy relationship is trust. As I have said in the first chapter, you're going to be taking a leap of faith on each other. You have to let go of all the traumas of your past relationships, like the PTSD you may have from an abusive or cheating ex. And you know what? She has to do the same. This is now an even playing field! If you can't trust each other then you will not be able to build a relationship that will last. Take that leap of faith.

Honesty:

This factor goes so seamlessly with the previous one. With

trust comes honesty, and with honesty comes trust. You must be able to be open and honest about absolutely everything in your life. This means financially, sexually, or with your future goals and ambitions. Anything that you try to hide is going to come out down the road any-ways, and it will hurt you if you're not open about it. This doesn't apply to just the bad, but the good as well. Be open about the road you see yourself going down in the future, the things you want for the relationship, and the person you see yourself becoming. Be honest with what makes you feel complete and happy, the things that you enjoy sexually, and the little things that make your day. Both of you need to have a transparent and honest relationship in order for it to work in the long run.

Mutual Respect:

Respecting each other's boundaries and personal opinions is so often overlooked. No matter how much you have in common, you're not going to agree on everything. That's okay! As long as you do not see a difference in opinion as a fighting matter, but a possibility to learn more about each other. You can even turn the difference in opinion into a playful debate. What's not healthy is attacking each other for a difference of beliefs. You should not be trying to change the other person's mindset on a subject, and then getting angry when your partner doesn't see things the way you do. Respecting each other's opinions builds a deeper love.

Great Sex:

Of course, great sex is important! Being with someone who you can be open with sexually is a beautiful thing. And you know what makes it easier to have a great physical relationship? Honesty. Trust. Respect. If you can be honest with them about your primal and physical desires, then they'll open up to you as well. This builds an even stronger bond with them. Having a genuine, deep connection and a desire to please your lover is one of the key things to great sex. A woman can tell the difference between sex that is purely lust-based and the actual act of "making love." Yes, it sounds cheesy I know, but it's obvious when the person you love appreciates every inch of your body. There will always be days where the scale of giving/taking tips more to one side than the other, but the balance of understanding each other's physical and primal needs is one of the best things that helps build a strong relationship.

Speak Positively:

It's been scientifically proven that speaking negatively about anyone or anything automatically creates a negative narrative in your mind about that person or thing. The same goes for your relationship! The day you start speaking negatively about your person behind their back is the day you need to re-evaluate your relationship. Go to them first with your issues; don't go to outside sources like your friends and family. You need to figure out why you harbor these feelings inside you in the first place. Negative words create a negative mindset and can lead to arguments and resentment. Resentment is a feeling that is almost impossible to overcome in the long term. Remember to always speak positively about each other no matter what!

Common Goals:

Having common goals and ambitions is a great part of building and growing together. It can be anything from business goals to religious beliefs. When you have something you are both passionate for, it will make things a lot easier for your relationship in the long run. Especially when it comes to financial goals, since it is statistically proven to be one of the biggest reasons why couples argue. Once you have something that you are both working towards as a team, you start to see how well you communicate and grow together. It can even be something as simple as a fitness goal or building a project together or reading the same book and talking about it once a week. Common goals and interests are a very important part of keeping your relationship going, and you can learn something new in the process!

Patience:

Having patience with each other is so important that it should be its own love language, if you ask me. Patience isn't just waiting for her to get dressed for a night out after you've already been ready for an hour. No, I'm talking about a different kind of patience. Patience that can sometimes even be painful, especially if it's being patient with each other's emotions. Being patient with her and with yourself as you heal from your past, being patient as you both grow together and work out the kinks of your personal differences. It is important to have patience for what matters to her, like her dogs, her family, her career path or her struggles. The kind of patience that evolves from an understanding that things won't always be like this, so enjoy the ride and support and help each other grow together.

Fight with Love:

No relationship is perfect; you're going to have disagreements.

The difference is that in a strong, lasting relationship, you learn to speak with love. This means that when you disagree, you still understand that you are mutually on the same team. The things you say are not meant to hurt your partner, but to speak your mind and present your case in a constructive way. When you realize that you only want the best for each other then you learn to disagree in a constructive and loving way. If you can't find it in yourself to speak with love, then take a 20-minute cool down away from each other and re-evaluate why you're triggered. Go for a walk or take a shower.

The key is to give yourself the space to figure out why

you're feeling the way you are in the first place. Give yourself one task after another to make the time go by, and you can really take a calm approach to figuring out your emotional state. She can do the same thing, too. Even in anger, it's a team effort. Once you've both reached a coherent point of cooling down, you can then explain to your partner in a more loving way why you were upset. This also requires honesty and respect, the main core pieces of the backbone that support the system.

Communication:

If you want a long term and loving relationship, then communication is key! It's the key to absolutely everything.

Great sex? Communication. Trust? Communication. Honesty? Communication. Don't know what to eat for dinner? Communication!

It's one of the best ways to keep your love open and flowing. If you've had a bad week and you're agitated about it, then you should be able to tell your love that you need some space or explain why you may be coming across as abrupt with her.

One of my favorite examples of this is the traffic analogy: If you're stuck behind a vehicle that is driving too slowly or driving erratically, you get frustrated and lay on your horn to tell them to get out of the way, right? Now let's say that the same car, driving the same exact way, is in front of you. Except this time, they have a "Student Driver" sign on the back. You're a lot more patient with them, because they've communicated that they are still learning how to drive and now that you know that, you will probably be more forgiving of their driving.

Communicating with your partner in every aspect of your life allows her and you to show empathy towards the situation. It also gives you both a sense of relief that you don't have to walk on eggshells with each other; she knows you're not particularly upset with her and you know she isn't going to take it personally as well if you need some time. Now you both get what you need, all because of that open line of communication.

Empathy:

Part of healthy communication is being able to empathize with each other. Basically, you should be able to put yourself in each other's shoes in situations where you feel like you particularly don't understand each other's emotions.

For example, you have a friend coming to visit from out of town and she might not be acting very excited about it. Consider some of the reasons she may be feeling that way, even if she verbally said it was okay for that person to come over. Pay attention to actions as opposed to just her words.

Compromise:

This is a form of respect, but it definitely deserves to be expanded upon and singled out. You can not have a strong relationship without being able to compromise. Let's face it, even identical twins have differences. Since you and your Bunny are far from being identical, you're going to have things you disagree on and you're going to have different ways of approaching those situations. Understand that you have to give a little every now and then, and come on, if you can't compromise, then you're not ready to share a future with another human. Each of you will have a difference in opinion and that's a beautiful thing, especially if you can communicate and come to a loving compromise on those opinions. You both walk away from it feeling respected and knowing you were listened to and heard.

CHAPTER 10

Accepting Your Bunny

I'm going to make this one short and sweet. Love her for who she is. It's not rocket science. If you love everything about her, but you don't like the career she chooses or the dreams she has for her future, then guess what? It's not going to work.

Think of it this way, like cauliflower versus mashed potatoes: you love a nice creamy helping of mashed potatoes, right? Yet you read that cauliflower is actually better for you. So, you go out, and order that side of mashed vegetables instead of the creamy potatoes you really wanted. And guess what? It's not the same. You don't love it, and now you're mad that your vegetable isn't a carb. Is it the vegetable's fault, or yours?

Creating expectations for your Bunny is the same: you can't date someone because of their good qualities or because everyone says they're the better option. You have to go with your heart on this one. If you want to date a model, a CEO, or an entrepreneur, then you have to know who you are getting into a serious relationship with. One day you decide you wish she had an office job and corporate health benefits, then what? You cannot try to change her after you get into a relationship with her. That's not her fault. You fell in love with her for who she was back then and now you've changed your mind? That's on you to decide if it's worth it for you to respect her decisions and love her or let someone else step in who will.

You admire your Bunny for so many of her qualities, and guess what? You are not the only person out there who sees her worth. Better yet, SHE knows what she is worth. A strong woman will know what she brings to the table. Some people value the cauliflower, some prefer the creamy mashed potatoes. Just accept what you truly want and embrace that instead of having FOMO for the other option.

Remember, she's an actual human being. You want your own beliefs, dreams, and opinions to be validated and heard. Of course, she wants the same thing. Trying to guide her in a direction that you approve of in order to change her is considered "controlling asshole" behavior.

One of the reasons that it becomes difficult to accept your partner for their true selves is that you're hung up on someone from your past, and you're comparing her to them. Once we move on from an old relationship, there will always be little things that we remember about it. It's human nature to compare the new to the old, but you can't support a healthy relationship on those comparisons. Maybe your past relationship was a fitness nut and you're happy to be with someone more relaxed now, but this means you can't expect them to have the same level of endurance that your ex had on an outdoor activity or sport. It doesn't mean that you want that other person back, but sometimes it's almost habitual if you were with your ex or hung up on your ex for long. Realize that the person you're with now or pursuing now is a completely different person, and they aren't responsible for the outlook you had on your ex.

If you find yourself comparing your Bunny to someone from your past or you find yourself wishing they chose a different career path because of your own reasons, it helps to sit down and discuss these things. Not the comparisons, of course, but their motivations. Work on being a part of the bigger picture and seeing things from your partner's side. You are not forcing them to change, but you're helping them work towards their goals by guiding them to be better. Get to know the whole story, or just listen to it again if you've forgotten why they're passionate about their path.

The grass isn't greener on the other side; it's greener where you water it. Like my Nana always said, "Love a woman for who she is or get the hell out of the way for the man who will."

CHAPTER 11

Digital Dating

All of the uncomfortable first dates that I've talked about have all been those in-person awkward first date scenarios. The dating world is transitioning to being more digital, which means online meetings are actually more common than you think. If meeting a complete stranger for the first time makes you feel anxious, then you might consider having your first date online.

There are a lot of pros to this kind of dating. The biggest one, for women, is safety. It's like a screening process before you get the big interview, right? She gets the chance to see you, talk to you, and feel comfortable. Most importantly, she's doing all of this while in a safe place. (Remember, the opposite of feeling "creeped-out" is feeling safe). There's not an awkward ending of wondering if there would be a second date, or even if there's going to be a kiss at the end. Also, believe it or not, I've personally gone on a super awkward first date. It was clear he wanted that end-of-the-night kiss, so I just kissed the guy to avoid him getting upset. I did this so I could safely get home on my own that night. It would have been a hell of a lot easier to have been able to find out there was no chemistry via a phone call or Facetime first, rather than finding out in person on a first date. .

The downside to the digital dating world is that there really isn't a rush to meet in person initially, and any relationship that is solely maintained online is very two-dimensional. There isn't a deep connection when a relationship doesn't have a physical aspect to it. The video chat sessions should be kept to just an initial meeting, instead of being used as a main form of communication.

Now, even as I write this, the entire world is on lock down and bars are closed (thanks to COVID-19). However, there are special cases where there isn't the option to meet in person right away. The biggest thing you want to stay away from is someone who is catfishing you or who is using you for financial gain. If you're looking for some beautiful woman to pay to chat with you online, trust me, there are plenty of them out there. Then again, we're here looking for our forever Bunny, not our web-based vixens.

You want to make sure that you can comfortably establish

a base of trust and compatibility before you meet up on the first date and going digital is a great way to do that! Just don't fall into that thirst trap of the online dating world. A woman who is genuinely interested in you will be more than willing to meet up, especially if there is real chemistry on that first video date. I hate that I have to even put this, but unless you have a monthly subscription to talk to her on a chat site, no woman who is worth your time is going to ask you for money. That's a scam every single time. Don't fall for it!

The reason these first-time-digital sessions are great is because you have the comfort of being in a place where you feel like you can be yourself. She also gets to be in the safety of her own home, and you both have the comfortability of ending the call if it isn't working out. This is a way better option than to awkwardly wait for a cab or the check at a restaurant, or even being pressured into a good-night-pity-kiss that you don't want. There's no pressure to keep the conversation going if it isn't working out, and there's no closing time to worry about if the date is going well.

Best of all, you get to pick the lighting and make sure she can see you from your "good side" right away! Just kidding,

but really, going digital for the
first meeting isn't a bad idea.

CHAPTER 12

Compatibility and *gulp* "Zodiacs"

Yes, this is a chapter on zodiac compatibility! I know, I know; you've already rolled your eyes so far back in your head that you can see behind you by now. I was skeptical about putting a chapter on this in my book, but I ultimately decided that I needed to add it in because zodiacs really boil down to one thing: predicting compatibility.

Look, no one wants to be labelled as "that person" when it comes to letting the stars predict and dictate your love life. (I could make a Professor Trelawney reference, but I'll leave the Harry Potter jokes aside). It's not a form of witchcraft or hocus-pocus, and there are a lot of women out there who believe heavily in it. However, what this boils down to is wanting to know if this potential relationship is really worth it or not.

Astrological signs go a little farther than just the cute, "what's your sign?" pick up line on the first date. Although a popular question to pop, it goes a lot deeper than just small talk.

The person asking the question is trying to not waste their time on a relationship that's doomed from the start. Whether or not your zodiac sign actually defines you specifically might not matter to you, but a growing percentage of the population believes astrology effects romantic compatibility. To be specific, around 66% to be exact. They're a popular belief because statistically and scientifically, there is some truth to it, whether you believe in it or not.

Let's just say that you really, really don't care about what the stars say about you. Okay, I get it; however, it's not about you. It's about her wanting to be comfortable, wanting to know more about your personality or your past without having to ask you a hundred intimate questions. Looking into someone's astrological sign is her way of showing interest and seeing if it would pan out.

Most people in the dating scene like to look at every angle when it comes to getting to know a new person in their life. By trusting the astrological definitions of the zodiac, it can help them feel confident in the direction that they're going. It's also a way for them to better understand themselves, and their potential relationships.

So basically, delving into your horoscope and your

zodiac usually doesn't come down to believing in the stars as much as it relates to not wasting each other's time. It's also a good sign because it means the person you're interested in is showing a long-term interest in you, too. You don't have to take it seriously, and chances are, she doesn't take it seriously either. However, I can guarantee that if she is interested in anything past the first date, she's doing her research on you. Yes, that also includes your zodiac. Ultimately, you need attraction and connection on that first date, and an astrological reading won't make or break it, but some people believe it's a helpful tool to support that connection.

CHAPTER 13

Taking Constructive Criticism

There's a fine line between criticism and constructive criticism. One of them causes you to drift apart and the other one stabilizes the connection between you both, and helps your relationship grow.

Dating is tough because it's mostly intangible feelings and thoughts, right? We're working with raw emotions here, whether we show it or not. That's why it's so hard when you feel like the person you love is being a bit too harsh. The bitter truth is that criticism is important, although rarely communicated correctly. We need constructive criticism in every aspect of our lives: work, love, and family relationships all require it. Yet, what do you do when the criticism that should help you grow becomes hurtful?

First, let's understand the difference between constructive criticism and abusive criticism. Something that comes from someone who genuinely loves you and cares for you will feel like a conversation on personal growth. It doesn't mean that it's going to feel pleasant, because no one wants to hear how they're failing. You can, however, tell that it's coming from a place of love.

We don't always come from that mature state of mind. Growing up, criticism came more in the form of bullying. It then became a deep-rooted insecurity of other people telling us that we weren't good enough. Kids don't criticize in a mature, nice manner. They see something that they don't agree with and blurt it out. Kids are blunt.

Fast forward to our adult lives and that kid that hates to be criticized still lives inside us. It takes years of development, growth, and political correctness to learn how to speak to another adult. Many people get defensive when they're being criticized.

In fact, check some of the top synonyms for criticism: disapprove, censure, disparage, complain, condemn. None of these are what we want to hear. So naturally we take it personally as adults even though we know that it can come from a place of love and positive intentions.

When we feel defensive about being criticized it's because we feel misunderstood or triggered. It leads to stonewalling, or refusing to answer or process information, which means you're afraid to feel vulnerable. It's not easy to become more comfortable with those feelings. It will take work and awareness. This is why the first chapter of this book is about handling your past and healing those traumas that can cause you to stonewall your partner.

Constructive criticism is a big part of healthy relationships because it's one step away from complaining, but it comes with a solution for the things that need to be addressed. It only becomes a problem when that criticism becomes a habit. Since the root of criticism is a negative one, it can pave the way for more abusive relationship habits.

Keep your ego in check: people who can't take criticism well have an issue viewing the bigger picture because their pride won't let them. Trust me, even writing some of these chapters, I've had to step back and take a big slice of humble pie. There are a lot of people who cannot handle being wrong or seeing their own flaws. Take a back seat and let the people in your life shine light on some things that can ultimately make you grow.

When it comes to constructive criticism in a relationship, the truly constructive ones will have everyone else's needs at the forefront. It's characterized by the flexibility of the alpha role and mutual concern for their partner's needs. Everyone who is involved is concerned for everyone else's needs, and it progresses the relationship forward. It's a way of growing together as opposed to a self-centered ego-driven approach with negative non-constructive criticism. The latter can be toxic to a couple, eroding away any positive feelings over time and leading to other abusive and problematic behaviors.

Being able to successfully provide and receive constructive criticism in a relationship takes a leap of faith. It takes a solid foundation of trust and respect to openly and effectively communicate, especially when it comes to a complex topic like criticism. As long as you continue to work on this sensitive topic then trust and growth can be achieved.

CHAPTER 14

Hop To It!

Of all the information I can give you, the most import-ant thing to remember is this: don't overthink it!

Seriously.

Educating yourself and researching ways to bag your Bunny already puts you years ahead of everyone else. You *care*, and that's a great first step to this journey. Get out of your own head, and just *do it*.

Overthinking involves dwelling on how bad you feel and thinking about all the things that you have no control over. It won't help you develop a new insight, problem solving skills, or self-reflection. Spending time in your own thoughts is only going to leave you sitting still on your ass and not doing anything to move your life forward.

One of my favorite riddles is the story of the three birds on a branch. Of the three birds, one made the decision to fly away. How many birds were still on the branch? The answer is three. Just because one had made the decision, doesn't mean it actually took action. So stop over thinking, and take action!

The next important thing to remember when you're out on your quest to bag your Bunny is to be kind to yourself. After a history of failed relationships and hard rejections, chances are that you don't have the nicest inner monologue. A lot of us don't have a voice in our head that is kind to us. Afterall, the old saying is true: you can't really love someone until you know how to love yourself. *This doesn't mean that you aren't worthy of love*, it simply means that while you're falling in love with someone and showing them the reasons why you deserve love, you should pay attention to those things too.

How are you going to expect someone to be kind and understanding to you if you can't even be kind and understanding with yourself?

Here's a little trick that I like to try when I notice that I'm not being forgiving to myself. First, think of someone in your life that you look up to or admire (for me, it's my Nana). Now, think of their life. Their hardships and struggles, right down to quirky or strong things that made that person into the one you respect.

Now, look at your own life. For me, I consider a lot of the things I've been through in my life to be baggage. In my eyes, those make me less lovable, they make me consider myself as "damaged goods." However, the very same hardships that my Nana went through in her life-time, I consider those to be her strengths. So if those struggles made the person you admire stronger, then why would they make you less of a person?

They don't. You aren't dam-aged goods. To someone, you are worthy of love, even if you had people in your past make you feel like you are not. You are strong.

When I find myself not being kind to myself, I try to remember that. It really helps shift the outlook towards posi-tivity and strength.

Being kind to yourself cre-ates an aura of confidence and compassion that you need in order to work on *yourself* first. If you're in a relationship where you feel secure, staying in it while working on yourself can actually promote personal growth. It's always possible to find yourself, be kind to yourself, and evolve.

Another thing to remember is that you can't play the blame game. Did you have a bad date? Did things not go as planned and you're disappointed? Don't blame other circumstances or people. When you throw the blame somewhere else, you lose control of the situation. To hold yourself accountable means to take ownership of your feelings and take responsibility for your contribution to the situation, whether it is good or bad.

The bottom line is that dating is uncomfortable for everyone. Even the most confident person has doubts. It's normal to get anxious about interacting with new people. We're all concerned about making a good first impression. If you let it control you, this fear of rejection and social anxiety will end up holding you back. This is where you can take ownership, remind yourself that you are worthy of all the love in the world, and "hop to it"!

CHAPTER 15

Direct from the Bunnies

Don't just take it from me! I chose some of my favorite shining examples from successfully bagged Bunnies that I know personally. Remember when I defined what a Bunny is? No, not just the bombshells that you'd find hanging around Hugh Hefner's home, although that is where I first encountered some of the most motivated and beautiful women I've ever met.

"The Bunny, to me, is a smart woman with her head on her shoulders, a sense of class, and a heart of gold."

Well luckily for us, they've agreed to exclusive interviews. Here are some advice and personal experiences to help you bag a Bunny of your own.

Leola, US Playboy Playmate:

Q: How did you meet your husband, and what was your first impression of him?

A: I met him while I was out with one of my best friends, you, lol! We went to a party at a hotel in south beach for Winter Music Conference. He was a mutual friend of one of our friends. My first impression of him was that I thought he seemed nice, but at the time he seemed like a typical Miami club promoter type. So naturally I didn't give much thought to it, but it wasn't like we were being set up on a date or anything. It was just a friendly atmosphere. We were just meeting in passing but he did stay the entire time we were there.

Q: How fast did your relationship progress after that? Did you start out as friends or move right into being serious?

A: We were pretty fast and furious in the beginning, to be honest. After about only a month of seeing each other, I moved down to Miami to be with him so we kind of jumped straight into a relationship and a friendship at the same time. I was living over an hour away and we really just wanted to be together, and moving in just felt like the right thing. I don't regret it at all though, the timing was crazy good. The first few years were pretty much party, party, party. We had a lot of fun times and created some awesome memories. I mean, it sounds like that would be the recipe for a terrible relationship but we've been together for almost 9 years now. We have tons of inside jokes and formed a really solid base from all that craziness.

Q: Was there ever a time when social media perception was

**important in your relation-
ship, either to you or to your
husband?**

A: No, never. Actually, I met my
husband right as my centerfold
was coming out. He knew all
about it and I made no mistake
in trying to hide it. Social media
at that time was a huge part of my
life and my job, and he had the
confidence to just accept that.
It didn't bother us or negatively
impact our relationship at all.

**Q: What would you say works
best for you both as far as effec-
tive communication between
each other?**

A: Honestly, never holding
back. Be kind, but don't hold
something back because you're

afraid it will hurt the other person's feelings. Just get it out in the open even if it might cost a little more friction up front. It's better than letting it fester.

Whitney, Top Model & Business Owner

Q: What are some things that you did in the beginning to establish a solid friendship with your husband? And how do you maintain those things today?

A: We had always been friends in high school and college. We were practically best friends, always helping each other deal with boyfriends and girlfriends. We also both love to cook and love to travel, and we joke constantly. We're just really close.

Q: Describe a time when you or him or both of you were off your game, or down on your luck. How did you pull the relationship through those times and what kept you anchored?

A: When we opened both of our restaurants, and many times in between, the stress has been overwhelming. Often we say that sometimes, one of us has to be stronger than the other. There are times when I feel like I can't do it anymore and he has to pick up the slack, and vice versa. He never falters in his love for me, which is something that I've never had before. We would get in fights and I would threaten to divorce him, but he never, ever did that with me. He held fast that he would never want a divorce, and they helped make me more confident and stable in our marriage.

Q: How fast did you go from "just friends" to a full-fledged committed relationship, and what was the catalyst?

A: When we reconnected, both of us were against relationships. We had been through plenty of failed relationships with crazy people and we just connected on that. We literally both said we would never get married. I told him that I felt I was too old for a boyfriend and I wasn't interested in titles. I just didn't put any pressure on it because

I had tried that before and it didn't work. Then, when I had to move back to London for a few months, I assumed that whatever we had was going to be over because of the distance. Instead, he asked me if he could come with me. I had never been with someone who took any interest in my life. That changed everything.

Q: We've all been through something that we define as "creepy" in the dating world, right? So what is something you consider "creepy" about a guy, or what is a time that you felt creeped-out when you were dating around?

A: The absolute worst is lack of personal space. Physically speaking, invading my personal bubble, makes a guy creepy. Seriously. Anyone who doesn't understand how close to stand to me has something wrong with them in my opinion. It just doesn't feel safe.

Mervat, Business Owner

Q: What is something unique or "dorky" that your man does with the utmost confidence, and how does it make you feel?

A: He gets on his tippy toes when we take pictures, and it makes me smile! He's shorter than me by an inch, he's 5'3" and I'm 5'4". Oftentimes other men will comment or laugh when I post photos of him with his toes. We both find it funny! It makes me feel so secure and proud that he truly doesn't let it bother him. He's very confident in himself and that's a huge turn on for me!

Q: What was the catalyst that made your relationship go into a fully committed one?

A: We had such a strong connection on our first date and surprisingly neither of us we were looking for a relationship – only non-judgmental fun! We were real with each other and this led to us spending an enormous amount of time together for the first few weeks. Then he went on a 6-week vacation and almost canceled because he didn't want to leave me. The "catalyst" was when he did leave… We spoke and/or text every single day he was gone and that drew us so close! He made me a priority. It was an incredible way to get to know one another and it showed me how much I meant to him because he reached out to me every morning and evening while he was away.

Q: What are some common goals you both have that bring you closer together?

A: We have similar health and fitness goals, we love to eat clean during the week and then binge and have fun on the weekends together. We're also both very motivated and innovative, so we have similar success goals as well. We work really well together.

Tawny, Disney Princess

Q: How do you maintain your friendship with your husband after 12 years of marriage, right down to the jokes and activities you both enjoy?

A: I think we started off doing things we both liked, but then we started going to things or doing things for the other person that we didn't necessarily like, or KNEW we liked. For example, I was never really into sports but my husband is a die-hard fan of pretty much any sport. So we started going to a lot of basketball games, football games, baseball games, and even though they still aren't my favorite things, I found the fun in them and learned to enjoy them too. It's important to find the things you have in common, but it's equally as important to be open minded to the things they love that you aren't sure about. You never know, you might actually be introduced to something you enjoy! And the same rings true for us, 12 years later.

My husband loves to golf and I would have never golfed without him. But I actually find it really fun tagging along in the cart with him, sipping champagne and taking a few "celebrity shots" and although my husband doesn't love going to church, he knows that's a big part of my life and joins me when I ask.

Compromising is key. You have to give and sometimes you take. It's all about finding that balance. Another example, my husband was 25 when we met. He hadn't been to Disneyland since he was 12. I told him if we're going to date, he better learn to love that place! I took him once back in 2009 and that was all it took.

Now, he's even more of a fanatic than I think I am! But I know that the first time we went, he was a little hesitant. It just goes to show that you have to have an open mind, try everything at least once. You might be surprised! Having too much in common with someone can get boring real fast. Balance is always a good thing.

Q: Did you two ever have a "just friends" phase, or did you go straight to dating?

A: I don't think we really had a "just friends" phase at all. We hung out a few times in the span of a month after the first meeting, but more so in group settings with friends, not really on a date. We had our first kiss a week after we met so there was definitely no friend phase. But that whole month I was still kind of unsure about him, not to mention, I was single so I was also talking to a few other guys at the same time. About a month after we met, it was my birthday. I was having a big dinner with a bunch of friends and I did the unthinkable: invited him plus two other guys I was talking to just to pin them all on each other! Crazy, I know, but it worked out. My husband was the only one out of the three that came, and he also brought all his friends to celebrate with me and my girlfriends and he just made me feel super special that night. That's when things changed for me and I decided to date him exclusively.

Q: Do you know each other's love languages, and how do you maintain them if they're different?

A: YES!! My love language is "Words of Affirmation" and my husbands is "Physicality" Two very different ones. It's definitely taken us a lot of time to figure each other out. I think in the beginning, you tend to treat them the way YOU want to be treated and with whatever YOUR love language is. But that's totally wrong. If that's not their love language, they're never going to understand it. So you have to do your best to start thinking like them and put yourself in their shoes and vice versa. It's the only way to practice and learn exactly what it is they want and need.

Q: What would be an example of effective communication in your relationship?

A: Just being open about how we're feeling. I tend to sometimes do things to just "make" my husband happy and I've learned that u can't "MAKE" anyone happy. So I've learned to stop saying "yes" all the time and express more how I'm feeling about it. My husband is working on that same sort of thing too. He likes to clam up when he's upset about something. But he's been a lot better about that as well. It's all about growing. You don't start off being the most perfect communicators for the most part. But the more you learn about each other and the more you learn what makes them tick, you start to figure it out. It's not just about communication but the way you communicate, and how you communicate. When we were first married, we used to snap at each other way more, raise our voices etc. But I think we have both learned to change our tones. *Tone of voice is so important.* Now, when it seems like an argument is brewing, I think we both stop, collect our thoughts, take a deep breath and then do our best to convey our points in a kind tone. Staying cool and calm is always the goal. But it definitely takes practice!

Jessica, Playboy
MX Playmate

Q: What was an example of a toxic past relationship that you had to overcome before you could fully commit to your new one?

A: I wanted my ex's love so much that I was willing to compromise who I personally was. Behavior I questioned and believed disrespectful in the relationship became the norm. But I wanted his commitment and love so badly I disregarded these feelings. I was so sure the way he loved me was the real deal because it was so deep and emotional. So many highs but the absolute worst lows. It was a constant push and pull of "I need you, I love you" "I need space, I need more."

There wasn't a happy middle ground with my ex, and I truly believe this was his own inner turmoil between giving and receiving love and his own personal freedoms. It wasn't until a long time later when things progressed further when I was dating the man I'd end up marrying that I realized how terrible that style of love and compromise was. Adam (my husband) showed me what a healthy love and relationship was. So much so that I questioned it for the first 6 months together of being wrong and ingenuine.

Before I dove into anything with the man who is now my husband, I spent a lot of time alone. I dated but it was like a sporting event for me. Fun, casual, nothing serious. I wanted more for myself at the time, I was focusing myself and energy in a way I hadn't in several years. My career in modeling was at its absolute best and I didn't want to put that on hold for any man. I had returned to a form of self-confidence I believe radiated in my work. I can almost pinpoint the exact moment with Adam when I felt so true to myself, like he'd seen every inch of me and wanted all of it. He accepted all of my quirks, all of my needs and all of my career. The ability to be beside someone that you can show the worst of yourself to and know they won't leave you, it is priceless.

I'm not easy to love, I'm a pain in the ass, and he accepted this, loved this and nurtured who I was. I'd never had some-one actually genuinely just want the absolute best for me, includ-ing allowing me to be 1000% true to myself and my desires and goals.

Q: What is the creepiest thing a guy has done on a date, or just in passing, when you were single?

A: When I was dating, my sis-ter thought it would be great to sign me up on a dating site because I was working so much and meeting a man wasn't my priority. She insisted I see what was out there. I decided to go on a date with someone she pointed out and "vetted" for me. After a casual dinner at a cafe by my house we walked by the beach and had nice conversation. However, it became more and more clear he was looking for an instant wife. I tried to explain how my career was taking precedence, but I wasn't ready to set time aside for the right relationship. Several hours later when I was home sleeping I received a nasty message about how "I wasn't really looking for a partner in life" and basically a death threat for wasting his time, and there have been a lot of creeps similar to him after that too.

Q: How do you both communicate effectively in your relationship?

A: In our relationship there is no holding back. Adam will forever know how I feel and what I'm thinking because I feel SAFE enough to always share this with him. I do my best to provide an open safe space for him to always tell me what is on his mind as well, despite the pain it may bring me. We have learned over time that holding back from one another only causes larger problems.

Q: Anything else that you can think of that makes your marriage special? What lets you know that your husband is absolutely The One?

A: I know I'm a special breed, I am extremely opinionated, emotional and goofy. I have my bratty moments and he takes it all with a grain of salt.... or tequila. But in all seriousness, he is truly my best friend. In a very crazy world Adam gives my heart a home. Every moment joyous and not, I love to share with him. When I felt like my world was crumbling, he reassured me that we were building a new world TOGETHER. No moment has been too big or too small for him. He's shown me what true love, companionship and friendship is every day. We cheer each other on daily and we pick each other up just the same. I love how I told him my dreams and he acknowledged me. Instead of questioning my abilities he asked how we could make them happen. There are no words to describe how wonderful it feels to know someone has true faith and love in you. Loving Adam is the easiest, and best decision I've ever made for myself. I want to hang out forever with him.